WHY THE SHIPS ARE SHE

WHY THE SHIPS ARE SHE

TERRI FORD

FOUR WAY BOOKS
NEW YORK

Editorial Office
Four Way Books
PO Box 535
Village Station
New York, NY 10014
www.fourwaybooks.com

Library of Congress
Catalog Card Number: 00 134377

ISBN 1-884800-37-8

Cover Painting: Christian Schmit
Book Design: Brunel

This book is manufactured in the United States of America
and printed on acid-free paper.

Four Way Books is a division of Friends of Writers, Inc.,
a Vermont-based not-for-profit organization.
We are grateful for the assistance we receive from individual
donors and private foundations.

ACKNOWLEDGMENTS

Grateful acknowledgment is made to the following publications
in which these poems first appeared:

Agni: "Agnes"
Crania: "BP Station Employee Restroom," "The Clothes of
    the Dead Episcopalians," "Common Dressing Room,"
    "I Am Joe's Ego," "Wedlock"
Conduit: "Fixation"
Forklift, Ohio: "Anger," "Armory Square Hospital, 1863,"
    "Masturbation," "My Heart Goes Out," "State Fair,"
    "The Nine Insights"
Incliner: "Sexual Peak"
Kumquat Meringue: "Predestination"
Licking River Review: "Exclusion," "Hitler's Girlfriend"
Marlboro Review: "When he drinks"
The Plastic Tower: "Riding the Texas Giant with My
    Brother Steve"
Southern Poetry Review: "Panty Raid," "Parlor Beauty"
Warren Wilson Review: "Stacked"

"The Beach of My Mom" first appeared in the anthology
The Beach Book: A Literary Companion ed. Aleda Shirley,
Sarabande Books, 1999.

I would like to thank *Forklift, Ohio* for including some of
these poems in two broadsides, "Hitler's Girlfriend" and
"Green Drowser," and in the cassette recording, *Six Deadlies
and One Sorry Ass.*

I am grateful to the Kentucky Arts Council and the
Kentucky Foundation for Women for grants providing me
solitude at the Virginia Center for Creative Arts, where I
finished this book.

For my families,
original and chosen since

CONTENTS

THE SOUND OF ARROWS KEELING

My Heart Goes Out   /3
Girlhood   /4
Exclusion   /5
Predestination   /7
Agnes   /9
Hitler's Girlfriend   /10
Wedlock   /11
The Brain of My Ex-Husband   /12
Float   /13

HARD CARDIAC HOSE

Lawnmowers   /17
The Nine Insights   /18
The Clothes of the Dead Episcopalians   /19
I Am Joe's Ego   /20
Amanda Sucks   /21
Riding the Texas Giant with My Brother Steve   /22

THE DEADLIES AND THEIR AFTERMATH

Envy   /27
Gluttony   /28
Sloth   /29
Pride   /30
Guilt   /31
Lust   /32
Depression   /33
Anger   /34
Avarice   /35

YOUR MOTHER'S LARGE WHITE BRIEFS

Your Sorry Ass /39
Panty Raid /40
Parlor Beauty /41
Common Dressing Room /42
The Beach of My Mom /43
Stacked /44
Sister Mary Dragnet /45
Interview /46
BP Station Employee Restroom, 2 a.m. /47
Masturbation /48

HOVERCRAFT LOVE

Valentine /51
Ballroom Dancing Class /53
Armory Square Hospital, 1863 /55
For the Love of an Anaconda Woman /57
Dating Young Men /58
Sexual Peak /59
State Fair /60
Crossfire /62
Fixation /63
When he drinks /64
The Bird Shows Its Bright Head /65
I die /66

THE SOUND OF ARROWS KEELING

My Heart Goes Out

My heart goes out, little urgent hoodlum, hardly home
nights. Its gutterings brief, rascalities
legion — looks in on the poker game, stoops

to breathe in deep of the hookah. My portable
hoopla, aimlessly
hit man, bait what sinks. It is Kung
Fu fighting, it is taking
names, it is taking

days in bed for it to come true. If my mom
pleads, it doesn't answer. Any boy's turtle slogging

lawnward, a harpy's riverbound bag
of new cats, ticks on the lips of the blind
man's dog. Tonight Sinatra's place, Hank
Williams' car, bereft
and hammered.

Girlhood

How happy we were to begin
to use scissors, to point them in jubilation toward
one another, because we were warned
expressly not to. Sharp, silver,
thrilling with glint, what relief

to jab and pierce those paper
snowflakes, snipping like Girl Scouts gone mad.
But before we were passive-aggressive, we were
passive and learned to make flowers
of our folded hands, quiet as souvenir birchbark
canoes balanced on bathwater. Blame me

for anything, everything. Damage me. How easily
the boat tips still.

Exclusion

We called her the Wailer, the girl
in 201 who sobbed each night
in the months we lived in the
single rooms in the women's hostel
the year I went to school in London.
It was a joke, the sort of college
joke, young joke, group joke humans make
about pain too near or deep. Deep
as the anguished animal cries
each of us heard in our darkness, more
benign. I remember the sound of
the underground train, its shudder
and pummel through the tunnel; it rattled
the windows so that my friends and I,
conversing, would have to shout our secrets
until the train passed. I wanted to see

what the Wailer looked like. She had dark
hair, of course a swollen face, and
hurried on paths, looking down.
I don't know what
became of her, I don't know
her name; I never spoke
to her either in the other world

of waning light in which our grieving
is for the most part private
and contained. Or maybe this world
is glass, and the rattled window
is the sound of arrows keeling

from the natives who know
the terms of your despair
and have several names
for your shame.

Predestination

I had a short-lived physical thing
with the bishop's nephew. We were young
and drunken, hiccupped and tiptoed hand
in hand past the nuns' closed doors
to his tiny room. Another time
he stole the bishop's station wagon by
wintry night to fetch me from my mother's
house. In those days I was pleased
to behave as though I were a girl
on a big screen who, despite the mount
of the musical score and the danger
and the audience yelling, couldn't
be warned: she couldn't hear you. Soon,

the bishop's nephew wrecked it all by saying
to me "plutonic relationship."
Still this incident foretold a lot:
how my mom would have to attend
the seminary since I had turned out
a preacher's kid; how I'd become
a drunk and marry all wrong; how I'd always be

in awe of the women who married Jesus,
their dark robes, librarian's shoes,
narrow rooms, locked doors. I imagined

their souls lined up as correctly
as those black shoes; I only knew
one nun ever who got tipsy and asked me

for a cigarette, and I liked her.
As far as I know, I fooled the rest,
God, and my teachers.

Agnes

I try to conjure up a young Agnes, but the only picture
I get is the one in *Lives of the Saints* who holds her breasts out
on a plate: the hated breasts she now
can miss she offers outward in concentrics, halo,

deep dish. Desire must be a terrible thing
like an egg, it must be round, protruding, near
the source. *Cut*, she said
to herself and ran empty, now
she is planed level as lawn or a surface of water. God
swims alone. His lake is rockless and full
of hooks, all the losses
sink. How she wanted

her deliverance, but she will miss her breasts, parental and
sexual. I will miss them — for this poem
is clearly not about Agnes, nor any other saint
that I know.

Hitler's Girlfriend

I might have been Hitler's girlfriend. Maybe
in a speakeasy the slow clack
of his lighter to my lifted cigarette, maybe Adolf
even had a joke. Once the henchmen
would have impressed me, the unusual
moustache. In my youth I might have borne
any insolence, might have taken the lack
of smiles for a sign of brute
and sexual strength.

And the long climb up toward convincing
the self: all hardships his hardships; I didn't know
whose trouble mattered, whose
regret. O the long journey
toward ordinary kindness.

There were those among the rows of Jews
on the black line of train cars
who were told they were going on holiday; women checking
their rouge. There were those among them

who began to understand: men sat
in the sway, in the dark, dark
pressing through
the night. *We sat on our suitcases and wept
like old women.*

Wedlock

One of us was always
harping, mostly
the same one. One

was condor, one
rock bottom. One of us took up
all of the air: angioplasty. One of us meant

to drop an anchor, but the red motor sank
into the sea. Hold me, said the one
hand. Cut me, said the other.

The Brain of My Ex-Husband

No 4-H cauliflower comparison here, no issue
of health or stalk. Not a large fish grasped
in a joyous Kodak: in shape more like
the tunnel the government plots to build
where protons careen off one another
like drunken go-carts. More like a lane
with penalty boundaries, where heavy balls hurtle
toward an end. A hard thing full
of small, a foot
of many bones in a boot. With length: a torpedo prone
in a museum, full

of itself, of its own
disuse. Black ice: a sleeve of steel, a door
racked with deadbolts, or the stiffening eel lying cold
on the shore. The flint

in the profile of his sleeping face, he whom I wrestled with once
in the dark.

Float

So the friend says you're defective, and you love the friend.
Do you float? So the man you love is silent. Put the
arms out. Still face up. All the lights go out.
All your ice is melting. You are still light. Your brother's
children have gone to school, he found his wife white
with her opened arms rivering blood. If she works
very hard, maybe in three years she can dress herself,
a chance that she can grasp a cup. She will never again
sign her name. So my brother lies down, but he sees her,
stunned and obscene where she could not
be reached. Close your eyes, I say, you can float.
Here is the sun on your face; here are your children.
Float, damn it, float.

HARD CARDIAC HOSE

Lawnmowers

They have to throng a long noise, have to ride
their black knees on the hymnals of golf courses,
throttled. They don't have to permit
the hard cardiac hose of the engine
to sing what it sings. Don't tell me all
that's under green; I can live. Once in a while

the heart stops mid-careen. Some whiles the moon
and the moonrocks that hailed
will stop across sceneries, pause over
swimming pools, sod rolls, hillocks,

gulch. In a little while all the machines low
in their least bays will head out again.
Nobody's engines art thou, no
thrombosis, each lawn is a sea, tender,
reliable, in lanes marked and unmarked as swimmer's
lanes on the lawn
where you read.

The Nine Insights

They play big band music behind placard stalls dandified
with felt musical notes. Their music is thoughtful
but friendless, as though they disliked
the part of practice that requires conversing, and all drove
separately to each gig and home, each
to his studio apartment with no messages blinking
on the answer machine, no girlfriends to call and comfort
after a desolate show with orange rinds stranded
in glass bottoms. They do not patter between songs
like news anchors; to see them dance in their underwear
is unimaginable; likewise describing to a girl
how the trombone's low notes make the mouth
vibrate. They play weddings, yet have no joy
in costume nor in crime; they cannot be
televangelists. They are the crepe-soled doctors

of swing; they are the egos of large
and nearly extinct poultry; any secrets they have
would bore me. Still I wait at the second table
for what they might teach me and my waiting

gets early, then blue,
and so to dark.

The Clothes of the Dead Episcopalians

Episcopalian Thrift Shop
Amherst, Virginia

Some of the dead wore unsuitable clothing: Avon fashions
and pleated chiffon, the cracked shoes
of high school. Some of the dead
wore lingerie, swimwear, shirts
from Camp Hornet. Some of the dead

were very small and wore light children's shirts
with the depictions of surfers intact and the anxious
phrasing. All around me, the things

of this world — their smeared
souvenirs, the hearty garb
of those who golfed, the twist

of their earrings and bookmarks. It's wrenching
at me now & later in my second floor window
where I lie awake with the cheap and infinitive
calls of bad birds. Say, how long

can these birds last? Let's sell off
their music. Let's take
the male plumage.

I Am Joe's Ego

Consider the Aqualung — it swells, recedes, a necessary matter
made with breath, animating as curtains do or fire bellows

emptied. Think of me plushbutted in the restaurant chair
you took for spare, where the couple meets and rubs — I bluster

there, and over the woman in bed, I am trumpet or piccolo, then
fanned batwing, slumbrous in might. Joe checks me as one checks
an airbag, lest I blow

growling through Joe collared, females
rolling eyes — Am I not large? which still signifies

good. Baldly I strut and jest when he lets
me out, fifth leg of the African elephant. Me terra

firma, Poo-bah, on whom Joe relies when, loping, he hopes
beneath her windows like any wolf, a teen

in unknowing. Thronged, he is daunted and needs
my swagger and pistol, the sound of my saloon doors

sure. Pause while I spit. Clear my way to chambers, I assist
at the side of Joe's heart, O thwartable
Joe, centralized, where he varooms, harpooned, voluminous.

Amanda Sucks

She sucks up all
of the ziti pasta, hydroelectric.
Slurps, perfectly
Hooverish. Her lungs blabber

lengths, incarnate. Amanda blows. She blows out
all of the gears on the lawnmower, speakers,
the blender; she blows the bagpipes and
the delicate glass, seen through, unrepentant. She's blown

a gill, she'll be adding a blowhole, she's blowing
up all of the plastic globes on the beach. There is

some joy, there is no lack
of air. When Amanda kisses you
she can hold your breath too.

Riding the Texas Giant with My Brother Steve

What low chicken taunts
have I risen to? Red rooster, beside
my older brother, joshing, pinned
bellywise by a steel bar; in ascendance,
clutching: Mom, I want
to be grounded. Blue and steeply
we are rising, small, and crest. No. Then fear

is vivid in the mouth, and I, I
who some actually come to
for calm, I shut my eyes and begin

to scream primal down. I'm four now, up
in the stone rotunda topping
Enger Tower, and my father is holding me
out in the air. It's a joke, anyone
can see, as my father's long teeth laugh
and I clutch and pummel, sobbing

above the trees and the powerless
antfarm tourists below. We are
not saved. Wind

and power, the usual guy sports, my brother
beside me now bellows wide and wild
as me, *Ahhhhhhhh*, long and low

as the dark I'm lost in. Banking
the corner, we speed on, lapse

and rush, I shut
my frightened face again. Today
is my birthday.

THE DEADLIES AND THEIR AFTERMATH

Envy

There is a snake. There is a snake on the tarmac.
There is a snake on the tarmac with
bad karma and it wants ritalin. Now.

I'm being pinned into my sister's dress.
It needles, it pinches,
I'm stuck. I am stuck and roarous, I am all
Alaska, I'm the Kodiak bear
chewing Alaska, or a barbecue
underwater. Singe —

I am in the desert. Nobody
saw me. No one
will ever see me   I'm half eaten I
am the fish in the claw or the claw
that burns   I am eating

or being devoured   I am some
snake breakfast   I am the snake
I am eating myself
  I log   I gorge
I am boring myself
I am sick

Gluttony

All summer long he feels himself fat,
who is not, but is buttless, angular. When he thinks
of ravenous, he dials me up, and pauses mid
nine thoughts for chomping. *Is there more*

of this soup? he says at my table
at the first spoonful, and rises and rises
for more hot bread. *I ate*

something today, he says shyly the next week.
I'm eating, he announces by phone. Carrots,
or maybe local oats, masticating. In my kitchen

he most unnerves me, reaching over near
for a leaf of romaine, a red berry's clean
cloven heart. I have lived with no one
for a long time. He puts a whole egg
in his mouth.

Sloth

Her fatal weaknesses are laxness and charm.
—Teacher's evaluation, graduate school, 1983

Arboreal, three-toed, slow — pretty much
the extent of my high school essay, which
I intended to be bent on this morning (morning's
mostly intended), but I am busy danging
my mother, who is banging
open shutters and *singing.* Or do I wake

in my room now — the heaps of deballooned
brassieres — who could tell; the phone
is making canary and I'm pillowed, groaning;

I would lay waste all day, consumptive
in bedjacket. My head is nose-diving, I am
all week-end, a little island
riotous holiday, I'm the radish flower
nobody eats. But it's Tuesday here, a jolt

of coffee, upright scenery, I could not be later
for work. Even so, hauling back the patio umbrella
from where it's blown overturned
in the alley, I want to sleep

in its open leaves, be tickled by luxe fronds
of big ideas. What a place to die! or be
photographed in, slack-jawed, hair blown, one arm
overhead, rich.

Pride

I have seen the peacocks feed in the orchard, bray, their blue
necks stretched, their loud tails down; I saw them come flying
down Perkins Road this morning, and I came too. I came

back. I have been
in the badlands, I have been
to Graceland, I was at the Land
of 10,000 Seashells where a morose bear
lumbered his kennel and sighing, sat.
I toured all of the major

man-made dams and hollered my whole name
into their pummel like a righteous parent,
mad. I was on my mission, a vacation

from missions of anyone
else, and as for saviors, I am
no backbone. I am my own
aching back. *When my wife says*
that she loves me, my brother said, *it's as though*
a child called me from across half

the world. I don't know
where I was. I make things
up. Heavy, blue, not accustomed
to flight, I'm back
and roosting up on the roof
with the other mutant farmer children.

Guilt

To right this boat, I would swim
a long distance in a rhythm that slows
to the rag of my breath where the lungs

unjoin. Who could swim with me?
Nobody. Who asked me
to swim this far? No one. Who could bear

these heavy arms? You. You would swim it for me
if you could. That is why I'm not swimming
toward you. Pull for me. Harder. I have to swim
all night.

Lust

For the Greeks, hell rolled under this world like a subway
without sparks. It was a river. And maybe still, prone
in bed nights, you can hear its talk, insinuations,
wet. When your hand cups down before sleep and the mouth

waters, quickening arch and slip, you
live there. When the train starts
in the distance its hurl and rattle for you

it is unappeasable noise, taking
and spending, no help until you
stand for it, stoke, engine,
piston, coil and your cryings out

subside. Hell to be in the river, angel,
and you're going to lie for it all night.

Depression

This is the crowding room
in the dark, where the old faucets
continue to drip, where you'll lie down
like a good dog,

stay. Oh, days, it seems, you've been
absent. So? You can't live

in love, off
the air. I

claim you. Lie
down. This is where

you have to
return. I suffer you
in my hundred
wet arms.

Anger

Woonsocket   puff adder   anaconda. Hiss
dropper   meal bolter   badger   pester
pestilence.   Hotheaded hurricaning
redheaded   blind   helmet   cuss cuss

cusser. Refusal. One-tracking   full-
speeding   diesel volume   smack &
palm dusting   blizzard-eating   motherfucking

steel-toed   drum-kicking
hailstorm. Throat slither root
burner pulsating tree-
splitting   golf-cleating   spine-cracking   beast

heater. Ate you. Over
you. Tooth. Force. Cigar ash.

Fossil. Ache.

Avarice

Ravenous yellow-eyed
junkyard dogs: what will
you take? You already have

a breast. You can't have
a lung or a bone or
one hand, and you can't

have her. We're lined up here, female
soldier to shoulder, and our shields glitter

in hard noon light. If I carried her uphill
on my knees, I could not lessen

one fire's edge. Fucking
cancer, call off
your dogs.

For Susan Methvin

YOUR MOTHER'S LARGE WHITE BRIEFS

Your Sorry Ass

Your doleful ass, your mournful ass,
your querulous and
plaintive ass. Your debtor's
prison ass, gorse
bog ass, your given up

already ass. Do I know it? This
tragic ass. This broken
arrow ass, this defeated defaulted
and fraying ass; your un-

entitled ass. Buck this. I liked
your screaming rhesus
monkey ass, your liontamer whip
and chair ass, your war

tribunal ass, its melee, garboil, gamma
rays. I liked your ass

busting into flame,
your emotive
contradicto ass. I liked

your robber
baron ass, your alluvial
ass. Liked your proud ass
trawling stern, liked your Cajun

joyous ass, liked your crowing
planetary ass. You were never
eclipsed. Bring that ass
back on home to me.

Panty Raid

It is 1974 and out the institutional open windows
of the college dorm, nylon bikinis in floral prints
are plummeting like the cheap bodies of birds. And then

your mother's large white briefs like a mainsail, like
a flag of surrender, begin a slow dancing down current,
cinematic, lithe. All of the faces
are turning up, hushed, like those
holding a hoop to save a child burning. It is the opposite

of being lifted into the sky
the way I imagined my grandfather ascending
after the long pain of illness: this large pair of underpants
falling forever on the startled face
of an undergraduate boy.

For Paula Snow

Parlor Beauty

Everybody's sister or mama owned some extension — a wig
or wiglet, a fall, false bangs. My mother had
a yellow satin Keep Your Hairdo pillow, which I'd ask
in some reverence to borrow on car trips, believing early
that better hair could change my life. Not knowing
what that was, I tried each incarnation: shag, pixie,
perm, frost. I raised an Afro not unlike Sly Stone's; I lacquered
a layer of wings until my bangs were a startled
surf's up. I wanted the volume up and out, bigger
than a TV set; I was asymmetric and foiled. And then

the audacious tinting began. Once, my grandmother told me,
It hurts me to see your hair like this.
Now at the beauty shop
we speak of Endora, with what bold gesture
she left a room, cast a spell. *To say it looks natural
would be a stretch,* one friend says with careful attention.
To say it looks natural would be an insult. I'm rising

from my helmet of hot air in my prison smock, the tint
on my eyebrows drawn presidential, oversize.
I'm Groucho Marx. I'm Hillary Clinton.
You're one of the Supremes, says the assistant: *Flo.* I
am reinvented again.

Common Dressing Room

Whoever you are, however bashful,
come in. There are those
who have come in
before you and stand
in support hose insupportable, and wave
the phototropic arms clambering

for sleeve holes, heads emergent
as flowers in science films speed
open, open. Some of them

are beside themselves — the wig
on the chair like a loose
Pomeranian, the living bra
uninhabited on its hook
on the wall —   Some preen. Some won't

look up. Some mothers prod
their daughters as though
they were dissatisfactory

starfruit. Whoever
you are, look here: it is lush
to be female, wild
with misery and dangers.

The Beach of My Mom

I know why the ships are she. I've got
this parent, striding down shore
like she means it. She does, swinging heads
of iceberg lettuce, purple cabbage. My mom
is a team, she's the strength
of blue, told off the Christmas tree
the year my dad left.

My mom is taking things out of my hands
to improve me. "Just *tell* me how," I say — apple pie,
hammer, needle — but she hasn't the words, asks
for the whatzit sitting on the thing
over there. This is how
she's always loved me — nonspecific, standing
too close like a basketball forward
in the too bright light, trying to take
the ball meant for mine, so when I look up
my moments of light are obscured by a reaching
of arms and a holler and all of the vast trees
are calling to me lest I injure myself, which I do.

My mother's not sleeping. She says
it's her change; for years she's charted every
outbreak: light spotting, old rust; or floating, how
she woke up drenched. She is endless, the beach
of my mom. I came from this
roaring. Against this current I'm wading out.

Stacked

Lean over, hon, the saleslady said,
having rent the everlasting
curtain. I step amidst a thousand pins
in the tiny room. What kind of a woman
goes in for the trade
of lifting and separating,
strapping, hinging,
the impinging? And the conferring
with the mother: A bit of padding? No!
She's twelve! They were against me,
the breasts, that is,
locked as I was
in the swells of my body.
My body thickened with verbs.
I listed. It wasn't the moon,
it was no revolution. They rose.
I was a storm at sea,
I was a ship who couldn't
get in, I was only in
the third grade when every girl
in my class in turn walked past
the misery of the new strap
across my back, and fingered
and checked and found the rumor
of my terrible difference
was all true.

Sister Mary Dragnet

What was the name of that far-off loopy nun
in the convent attached to our hostel
off Kensington Square? One day she chased
our hostel's warden, Nancy:
gaining on her, she sprints and with
a new use for the wimple, bagged
said warden like a chandelier, announced in
triumph, <u>I am the Duchess</u>

<u>of Sardinia</u>. Sadly, she was guarded
after that by more burly sisters, but maybe she found
in that watching some theological comfort, some parallel: even
the sparrow watched, etc., although her notion of God
may have then been bent. Think of God

as a papa driving; now think
of his thatched arm, extended
to whack. Those red-nosed

avenging sisters, surveilling
the hazards of breakfast
in their habits the color
of heliotropes.

Interview

He wants to know whether poets conjure
the great childhood scenes in order

to replicate feeling.   I stare.
Then answer, No. More like restraining

a herd of wild buffalo. And I remember
how the town in Wyoming — Chugwater — came by

its name: how the Indians drove the stampeding herd
to the cliff's edge, how the buffalo fell

in the river to drown, and took deep sobbing
breaths in the water, dying —   No, my feelings

have always been with me.

BP Station Employee Restroom, 2 a.m.

Here's the diagram. Here's
what a sawed-off shotgun
looks like. Here's

a Derringer, here's
a Colt. *Here are some words*
we used for drunk: Smashed. Trashed,
and bombed. Do not keep
any large bills on hand
after midnight. *Here are some words*
we use for kill: Hit. Taken out.
Elimination. Snuffed. Offed. Knocked
off. Keep the lot
lights up, as well as

inside. *Here are some words*
we use toward love: Crush. Flame.
Arrow. Torch. Fallen. I

fell. Maintain eye
contact with each incoming

person. Greet them. Hi.
Hello, chief. Buenos
noches. Hey, buddy. *Nobody*
move. Hello.

Masturbation

Body must have a ratchet, must have
its own racket, mine its own tungsten, tubers,

ore. Four times daily, so
said the last one, made

me sore. So shall the body
body jump for its long

chords, ride down the bell
rope, church up my own

hips. Hammock says the long
pipe, Tree sighs the drum, Balance
sings the one foot smart

to the ground. Oh speaks the loud
out, Oh sings the choir, Yow grins

the green drowser not
in jail. Happy? says the one
breast. Very, says the palm. TERRI

says my body body most
at home.

HOVERCRAFT LOVE

Valentine

Hovering insectile love. Fretful love, every
two mile check-up love, nerve pill rope-end indecisive highly
diagnostic love. Bracing love. Speedy

love. Medieval leeching what ho troubadour head-
lopping dulcimer lost
ark love. Manifesto
love. Give up the throne
love. Love as truce. Tectonic plate
rearrangement love. Ultimatum bad

dog love. Ziplock
suffocation love. Bottom
feeder plankton love. Trophy preener
improvement love. Pink pluming
hope burning diary teen
reversion love. Blurt
out love. Perpendicular
gridlock love, hall
monitor love, detention love. Bad
press love. Half-Nelson Gladiator
headlock uncle *you* say it blood-

spitting hard-breathing down
for count head
injury love. Log-rolling jolly
motion river gusto wet and
galvanized love. Sympathetic

Red Cross love. Sinatra, Iglesias, Don Ho, Yo-
Yo, Dvořák, Monk Chant, Yanni love. Not entirely
believable love. Wild
love, burned at the stake love, iron
lung love, bone marrow pacemaker
toupee love. Love in remission,
amputee love, Federal Witness
Protection love, in hiding subtext
Morse Code spy love. Revisionist

love. Open book test
love. Boundless applause in the front
row love. African trumpeting large
flap love. Stealth Bomber
love. Slow me down
love. Keyhole light
love. Pebbled
bird's egg love. Name it to
your face love, woke

up love, count on it
stouthearted no-leak no-fault
high octane 911 in the daylight unashamed
long haul fearful but right here intergalactic
Hovercraft love.

Ballroom Dancing Class

It's like hoping for God, my friend told me
when I spoke the name of the boy
I hoped for. Thus began my wrangle
with romance at age 14, my white-gloved hand
into any partner's anxious palm
at the country club on Thursday nights. We counted
out boxsteps, hurried, bluffed, miscounted: even

our shoes stammered and flushed. In what
far dream would the teens of Duluth
need to know how to mambo? Under eye
of varying sets of parents, our changing
chaperones, we chose or muttered assent to

our partners, and with the same pained boys
I sat behind in science, surpassed
in English, I attempted

to dance. It was all
impediment, halt and muster: until
the Thursday evening in bitter December

when the boy with the French last name
asked me to slow dance, the Chosen One (yes,
God) chose me, and wrapped his arms
around my ignorant body, held me near

and nearer: I closed my eyes. O hankering, pine,
elation. Did we even speak?
in what language? In that night,

in his arms, I forgot
my feet: my life
was wings, wings were all
that mattered: the sons
of angels gliding low
over the iced pines of Lakeside and
I in my body began
to open, to bloom
and burn.

Armory Square Hospital, 1863

The limbs came off. All day
they sawed in their stained
white coats; it's what surgery
meant, soldier — the arm
comes off, the legs

come off: where you are wounded, so
shall you be freed, and the legs
and the arms of the teenaged
and free, these limbs shall be carried

out to the grounds, these limbs
shall be piled up out
on the grounds, these limbs
should be buried beneath
the ground, but sometimes
the animals roust in them first
and eat them.

Trollope fainted. Whitman assisted, cutting
his own hand, and cradled the young men
and kissed them. Love for him
was a convalescence, a rigid pain, roused
devil of fever, war
in a sheet. Later, he removed himself
as they slept, emerging into pure night
where he walked beneath

a wet moon. The rain

came down, everything
came down, the rages of love
suffused, complete.

For the Love of an Anaconda Woman

To be with her, as many as ten men
anacondas will wrestle with her and each other
for weeks in a slow breeding ball. They look
like a moving circle of bike tires, adjusting
their claims. They look like a bad dream

of embrace, this global
grip woo, although (come on, fellas) her strength
is the mother of strong. Still they writhe
with her, licking
the air, so legion and so
single-minded: can these perps

be far from us? Their mouths
full of needles, wide
as bejesus, sleeping

in the hyacinth marsh. Somewhere I hope
there is one with my name, tetchy
and muscular, seething off
toward the cormorants, loved,
overloved, loaded
with small triggers.

Dating Young Men

Bravely they tap dance, roosters
on vaudeville. Without fear
or knowledge, they strut
their red craniums and flap, winged things
who trepidate in approach.
O bravado, pathos,

endearing edge. How they thrash about,
impressing, blind as a boxer with a face
swelled shut, still swinging
at they know not what,
having forgotten to check
for impact, for softening,
bruises, to listen. Mired

in themselves,
their longings touch

a part of me uncharted.
They disclose all
of their partial travels,
unsuffered. Travel me
in your unreliable car, kiss me hard
by the moon. What we need

can't keep.

Sexual Peak

Behold the bagboy at the Piggly Wiggly: how willingly
he bobs, long limbed, defers, charged
and anxious, Adam's-appled, perspiring
a little. "In the back
seat, ma'am?" Yes,
in the back seat. Your longings
could unstoke and fan themselves in a breathless
dewy dark, decreasing him like a new
road map, your hands in the hanked hair
of a boy whose name you just nabbed off
a tag on his apron. Bechance the limpid-eyed

record store clerk, the mechanic who, manful, expounds
on formulae, oils by numerical, lubes — *I die, Egypt,
die.* And likewise beware
the paperboy — he doesn't drive yet (but with what
red burns you'd dare to turn him —). Begone with

the fuzzy men you could not
get rid of; the men who read
science fiction; beware of your old friends
in this new glint

and seize; do not begin on your gay friends; beware
the past bodies through whose discarded phone numbers
you fork with such speeding and unreasonable

tines. You're alone, your two hands
on the gilded spine
of an open book, Catwoman, Milquetoast, world
with tonight's end, so what, amen.

State Fair

Blue block sunglasses like seen on TV,
lifetime guarantee, five bucks. Tomatoes
bigger than Buicks, red
as a surgery; tattoos of inked snakes in bloom
sidling down
the halter tops. This

is the kingdom of large and vulgar. Why
don't you take a stroll
down the midway? Toss a ring, win
a pink and bulbous
dog; buy a ticket for to see
the misshapen: you'll feel better reviewing
your own nude body tonight, or grazing among
another familiar. Children weep here
with stains on their mouths: they want

to be tall enough to ride
their desires. How can I tell them
desire is a big dog who slathers; desire
is a Ferris wheel that halts
and rocks; desire is no ticket and easily

spent? It's the dark man who cornered me, gliding,
in a shoe store in Tijuana when I was ten,
the tonguing man who fingered
and grappled. I went into myself
like night-blooming cereus.

But of course one doesn't tell kids that; in truth,
I turn with the gesture that reads: Dismissed. Look: desire

is grist. Use it for power, strong arm
the boys. You run with them, and show
what you want. Later, repose in the bath,
slowly smoking a clove cigarette.

Crossfire

I would not call my husband back, who never walked
no ocean's floor. I would not lower down
my flag. I may not lower
my flag again. If I stood before

a burning ship and talked of fire, he saw
no fire, or else I must have set that boat to burn. No more. Not

to be woken by his wanting to say, beery
and sorry, that I was too good for him; or wanting
a fuck in the ass. Please. Baby. Lifeboat, white

boat, set him out. Whose wife was I? Where
was I?

Fixation

As soon as he starts in with the kissing, I think
of geometry, how its many faces divide, subdivide in
unstoppable certitudes and of course that is
reductive. I think of Einstein
on the beach, that famous hair
blathering, the endearing whiteness
of his legs, elemental, and what he said once:
Why is it that nobody understands me and everybody
likes me? I hear hounds crashing
through the brush. Am kissing
him back. This physical landscape attaining
such needling levels of noise and of danger, I want to hover
above the trauma of bodies, leave
this room or transfer as out of a class to

another poem — a poem wearing huaraches
and snoring — but I'm being pulled under by other
wants in the throat of me, belting, gravitational. Do not think
of the active underlanguage of fuck, of shucking
or muddy, and stuck. Say no low words, not
lotion, not mount. Pretty soon I can stop this
with the mouth I use for interruptions and sit in my hands

over here. So. With this poem the held breath of the page
begins. Now the landscape is getting
some sky, some constables, a bird,
and some insistence one sees in clouds whiffing over
the pare of a moon.

When he drinks

I am left on shore when the barge
shoves off. I am the man in iron shoes, tamping
down wet concrete. I am a dog

in the pound, I am orchards oppressed
by rain, bird feathers, blood,

refrigeration, oar
lock, ice. When he tries

to be absent, I'm like Whitman fallen
in his locked bedroom, unable to move
or to call out. I don't stand

for anything, back to the locked
sodden room of the kid

that I was once, whirring,
passed over,
out

The Bird Shows Its Bright Head

Say she's divulging a dream in a room
and it falls on her, the red nervous
bird, just as she's saying, " — so
I kissed him." Her whole chest
goes red — stimulation, baby — simulation.
It beats on her and in her, the wild
tomahawk of its head. Is she going
to wing off right here?

She wants to, in fear, in love. But in life,
this story goes on with the constant alignment
of two friends alight and electric, two bodies

dipping and leaning and cupping, two mouths laughing
and watched by each other, and they could
and they might but do they; no, tonight, again,

they do not. Again tonight, all night they have been
horse thieves, awhooping and thumping   rope   boot-
deep in flank shudders   gallop   the sound
hoof-hard on the night tribal ground. Again tonight

each returns to a bunk, and watches the moon
slip into its other, safe country.

I die

and offer my body to science, but science
refuses me. The body is not
indignant; it ticks off a list of things
long done alone: the ritual
cigars, the poems, sit-ups, love
in the supine, most
of the showers (the body remembers, slick,
the breasts being polished). But science says
Not her in fact because I am too
many people, I am overpopulated. I am partly

my father announcing intentions to now use
the sandbox, I am my mother calling
across boutiques, I am partly my brother
being struck by his wife, I am my sad sister
staying home tonight sick. I am my grandfather
caught in the bar's back room with a woman who is not
his wife, being beaten outside by his two
eldest sons: now my father again, landing
the last kingly blow. I am my grandmother
frantically answering sweepstakes. I am my aunt
lunging after her husband with knives, with scissors,
I am running with scissors, I am literally never

prone on a table beneath
a white sheet. I am geared in my car up to
tropical temperatures, I am passing the elegant
long-lashed llamas, I am in
the tropics, I am dying, I am being
held up by wings, I see now at last
all that rug crying for nothing, I was never

alone, I was much beloved, I had a hundred
voices in me. Earth, will you

have me; snow, I'm a slut;
beach me, take me, mouth
me down and lift my red dress
gently. Take all of
my souls. Oh we promise
to sleep.

Terri Ford is a graduate of the MFA Program for Writers at Warren Wilson College in Swannanoa, North Carolina. She is a recipient of grants from the Ohio Arts Council and the Kentucky Arts Council, as well as the Kentucky Foundation for Women. She was the Ohio Arts Council Writing Fellow at the Fine Arts Work Center in Provincetown, Massachusettes in the summer of 1999.

Terri Ford performs her poems at venues around the country. She performed as the First Voice in Stage First's production of Dylan Thomas's *Under Milk Wood* in Cincinnati in 1997. Currently, she is collaborating with Uncle Glockenspiel, who makes a lot of noise to accompany her poems. For six years, Terri ran a poetry reading series in the greater Cincinnati area.

Truly the Glory of the Continent, Terri Ford lives triumphantly in Cincinnati. She is a total spice rack.